SCOTLAND
Birds of Prey

Des Thompson, Helen Riley
and Brian Etheridge

LOMOND
www.lomondbooks.com

Scotland's Birds of Prey

ON THE LOOK OUT

Where to begin? Look to the sky! Can you see something moving – is it hovering, flapping heavily, soaring in upward circles, gliding, diving or even stooping at breakneck speed? What are the wings like – are they broad, with finger like tips upturned, narrow and kinked half way along, pointed or blunt at the tip? And the wingspan – can you gauge if it is half a metre or even a massive two metres wide? Is the tail fork-shaped, wedge like, long and slender, short and stubby, or just like a fan? Can you hear anything? The calls range from barking, mewing, screeching, chattering, cackling, howling, whistling and even whining, given loudly, softly, rapidly or slowly, often repetitiously, and sometimes in bursts or at random. And what about the colours, textures, patterns and shadings of the upper and under body – the wings, tail, head, throat, breast and belly – which tell us so much not just about the identity of the bird, but also its sex and age?

So, up there, if you look closely and carefully, even distant specks can quickly become a male or female, juvenile or adult – a common or perhaps even a rare bird. Birds of prey consist of two unrelated groups or 'orders' of birds: the hawks, eagles, kites, buzzards, harriers, ospreys and falcons (the Accipitriformes) and owls (the Strigiformes), collectively called raptors. All have one thing in common – they are predators, typically taking live prey – though some (rarely owls) also scavenge and subsist on carrion when it is available. They are hunters, and the word 'raptor', derived from the Latin verb *rapere*, to take by force, reveals the nature of these birds. They hunt by wing, sometimes just a metre or so above the ground, or from perches, and at times by stalking or making surprise attacks using a boulder, hedge, ditch or building as cover. These are the top predators – superb indicators of the health of our countryside – and reflect the size and diversity of their prey numbers, as well as the condition of the food chain. Fun to watch, they engender admiration, excitement, enjoyment, but

Golden Eagle:
In the eastern Highlands golden eagles breed in Scots pinewood habitat, with a huge nest in an old tree used over many years. This eaglet has fledged recently, with the black tail band and white base revealing a youngster in its first year.

Goshawk:
The elusive 'phantom of the forest', the goshawk, seeks out undisturbed mature woodland in which to build its bulky stick nest. Despite preferring seclusion in the breeding season, the goshawk spends much time hunting open ground in pursuit of hares, rabbits and game birds.

White-tailed or Sea eagle: There are eight species of sea-eagles around the world. The white-tailed eagle which occurs in Scotland has the widest range – extending from Greenland eastwards across Europe, through northern Asia to Japan. In North America, the bald eagle is a very close relative.

they can also cause discord, especially when they prey on wild game or livestock.

Here in Scotland, with a great range of locations and habitats, we have one of the best places in Europe to watch birds of prey. At least twenty-three species nest here, and several more visit us on migration, as non-breeders or vagrants.

EAGLES AND OSPREY

The white-tailed eagle or sea eagle is the largest bird of prey in Britain, and its presence in Scotland is one of the great conservation success stories. It became extinct in Britain in 1918, but following international collaboration to support painstaking reintroduction programmes, Scotland had a remarkable forty-six breeding pairs in 2009 (producing thirty-six flying young). Found in a few sheltered sea lochs and islands in the west and northwest Highlands and Islands, this vulture-like bird was known in ancient times as the 'Erne' – Anglo Saxon for 'the soarer'; today, some visitors liken the large female to a flying barn door!

Majestic and powerful, the golden eagle reigns supreme in our remote, wild hills and glens. Numbering around 440 breeding pairs, this imperious bird nests on rocky crags, sea cliffs or ancient Scots pines (with some nests in use for several decades). Difficult to see except when soaring, eagles may appear only fleetingly over a high snowy corrie or towering rocky rampart. Sensitive to disturbance they may breed for twenty years or more if left alone.

The osprey is sometimes called a fish hawk, as they feed exclusively on fish. The numbers of this summer visitor have reached around two hundred nesting pairs in Scotland. The osprey's still-recovering population began with a single pair breeding in 1954, at Loch Garten, Strathspey.

BUZZARDS, HONEY-BUZZARDS AND KITES

Frequently mistaken for golden eagles, common buzzards have a wingspan only half the size of an eagle's. Now living up to its name as our most numerous bird of prey, the common buzzard is recovering its range as it spreads into areas where it was formerly present, but removed through persecution. Our other breeding buzzard (in name only, it is more closely related to the kites) is the rare and secretive honey-buzzard. Up to 15 pairs nest in Scotland – making up approximately a quarter of the UK population. With us only in spring and summer, this migrant gets its name not from eating honey but from its ability to find and then dig out wasp nests, with the grubs providing most of its food.

Osprey:
With a new layer added to it each year, the osprey's nest can reach mammoth proportions, sometimes leading to its collapse in wet or windy conditions.

The red kite is yet another conservation success story. Following their reintroduction to Scotland in 1989, numbers have grown steadily to at least 149 pairs in 2009 (with 234 young birds fledged). The first 'release' site was the Black Isle, near Inverness, followed by further releases in central Scotland, Dumfries and Galloway, and on the outskirts of Aberdeen. These buoyant birds are a delight to watch, with the constantly twisting forked tail providing a spectacle of manoeuvrability.

HARRIERS AND HAWKS

We have two breeding harriers. The hen harrier is a predator of heath and bog. The two sexes are strikingly different – so much so that historically people thought they were two different species. The male is pale grey with

Marsh Harrier:
Like the osprey, the marsh harrier is a summer visitor to our shores, with most of the breeding population spending winter far to the south across the wetlands of West Africa.

Sparrowhawk:
Populations of
this plucky hawk
plummeted during
the 1950s and 1960s
due to the food chain
being exposed to
toxic agricultural crop
dressings – leading to
crashes in some eastern
counties. Their numbers
only began to recover
following the banning
of certain pesticides.

black wing tips, contrasting with the larger brownish female, which has a white rump and barred tail feathers, giving her the popular nickname of a 'ringtail'. Numbering around 630 pairs in Scotland – by far the bulk of the British population – you may have a treat in early spring if you see a skydiving pair soaring and plunging in rollercoaster flights. This fascinating bird sometimes nests in harems, with some males on Orkney providing for three or more females (one exceptional male had seven!). Sadly, hen harriers have long been subject to percecution, and in England this is regarded as the most threatened of all breeding birds with only 6 pairs in 2009. The marsh harrier is one of our scarce raptors (with only eight to ten pairs in Scotland – far fewer than the 350 or so pairs in England), and breeds in a few coastal marshes. The largest of the harriers, these slow-flying birds are similar in size to a common buzzard, for which it is often mistaken.

The sparrowhawk is often seen around gardens or parks, dashing over a bush or hedge from a near-ground flight, the doyen of 'surprise' attacks. This supreme predator often pursues its prey on foot – rushing far into the thicket to make a kill. Nesting mainly in mature woodland and preferring coniferous trees, there are 8,000–12,000 breeding pairs in Scotland. Its close relative, the goshawk, is almost half as large again, and a much more elusive forest dweller. The size difference between the sexes is huge, the wingspan of the male being crow-sized and of the female buzzard-sized (in all of our birds of prey, except barn owls, females are larger than males).

Numbering about a hundred and thirty pairs in Scotland (roughly the same in England, and around two hundred pairs in Wales) the goshawk is a powerhouse raptor, with the female taking prey as large as hares and wild ducks. Another of our 'comeback' predators, exterminated in Britain by the late 19th century, this became a regular breeder from the mid-1960s – in many places following the 'escape' of falconry birds.

FALCONS

The falcons are small to medium sized, with pointed wings and streamlined bodies rendering them agile and speedy. The word falcon is derived from the early Latin *falx*, a sickle, and later Latin *falco*, a hawk. The peregrine falcon is the fastest animal in the world, often striking down birds after breathtaking stoops – recorded at near 200 mph. Nesting across most of Scotland, we have around 540 pairs – a third of the British and Irish population.

About the size of a blackbird, the merlin is our tiny falcon. It nests in the uplands, spending the autumn and winter by the coast. Handsome and pugnacious, the merlin feeds mainly on small birds and large insects caught in the air after dashing chases. Scotland's 800 breeding pairs make up just over half of Britain and Ireland's population. Our rarest falcon, the Eurasian hobby numbers no more than a couple of pairs nesting annually, though there are just over two thousand pairs in the rest of the UK. A swift-like predator (but almost double the swift's size) hobbies feed mainly on insects for much of the year, but switch to small birds when breeding,

Merlin: The merlin's nest is typically a shallow cup, scraped in the ground, in deep heather.

Kestrel: The kestrel's ability to remain absolutely stationary whilst hovering is unique amongst British birds of prey.

snatching their prey on the wing. We may see more hobbies if their range shifts northwards due to climatic warming, though presently there is just a handful nesting north of the English midlands. The kestrel, our most familiar raptor, is now causing most concern. Nesting across Britain, kestrels are declining across Europe for reasons far from clear, but possibly related to the use of some rodenticides. Kestrels feed mainly on voles and typically nest in

Peregrine: Breeding across five continents, peregrines are the most cosmopolitan of all falcons.

Short-eared owl: Always avoiding closed woodland, the short-eared owl haunts the open hill and moorland.

abandoned crows' nests, though will use a scrape on a cliff ledge or ruined building, or a tree hollow. There are around 7,500 breeding pairs in Scotland – possibly a fifth of the British population.

OWLS

The five nesting owls in Scotland are predominantly nocturnal, and numbers fluctuate over a set number of years in response to cycles in their small mammal prey, especially voles. Tawny owls are the commonest, with around six thousand pairs, and numbers have increased over the last decade. Interestingly, they are absent from the Outer Hebrides, Orkney, Shetland and large parts of the far northwest Highlands, where any 'hooting' birds heard at night are noteworthy. Little owls are the rarest with probably less than ten pairs – a fraction of the British population estimated at ten thousand pairs – and all of ours breed close to the border with England.

Barn owls are a delight to see, and Scotland's nesting birds are the most northerly in the bird's world range. Once common on farmland, there has been a wide-scale decline in numbers. The British population numbers around three to five thousand pairs, with the current population estimate in Scotland likely to be at least 500 pairs and possibly as many as 1,000.

The long-eared and short-eared owls are our two remaining nesting raptors, and both are poorly understood. The long-eared owl typically nests in trees in old crows' nests, and is strongly associated with woods where it feeds on field voles, wood mice and rats. This is the easiest bird of prey to overlook, with the adult spending daylight hours perched close to a tree trunk. Their calls are distinctive, with field guides describing the song as a deep, coo-moaning 'oh' repeated every two and a half seconds, and the chicks begging with loud, heartbreaking and plaintive 'pee-eh' calls (likened to a rusty iron gate) audible at over a kilometre from the nest. There are an estimated 600–2,200 breeding pairs in Scotland; it is scarce or

absent in the northwest Highlands, the Outer Hebrides and the Northern Isles. The slightly larger short-eared owl can sometimes be seen feeding by day, especially in the late spring and early summer, and is most likely to be encountered over moor and heath. It nests on the ground in young forestry plantations, tall heather or rushes. Numbers settling to breed vary markedly from one year to the next and in line with the abundance of their main prey, field voles. In the best years there may be as many as 1,250 nesting pairs in Scotland but in poor vole years only a few hundred. It is absent from Lewis, Shetland and large parts of the northwest Highlands (and, curiously from Ireland, with the exception of a couple of pairs). If you are lucky, you may witness their wing-clapping song flight. In its wavering flight, this rather special owl can appear to be rowing in slow motion, with the pale, yellowish-brown appearance hinting at its scientific name, *Asio* (ear tuft) *flammeus* (flaming, fire coloured).

Long-eared owl: Varying numbers of migratory long-eared owls from Scandinavia and Russia visit Scotland in winter, arriving across the North Sea in late October and November to enjoy our milder weather. They form daytime communal roosts in woodland, occasionally numbering up to 25 birds.

OCCASIONAL VISITORS

The gyrfalcon, an occasional winter visitor, is the world's largest falcon, feeding on ptarmigan and collared lemmings in its arctic and tundra breeding grounds. The rough-legged buzzard, another winter visitor, feeds here over lowland farmland with open woods and rough ground fields;

Snowy owl:

In Scotland, most sightings of the snowy owl have occurred in Orkney, Shetland and the Outer Hebrides. Originating from breeding grounds on the tundra of arctic Eurasia, some individuals have stayed for prolonged periods – feeding on rabbits and medium sized birds.

Osprey:

A marvelous portrait of an osprey on the Spey Bay, adopting a typically upright pose. This bird may have migrated back and fore to West Africa over many years, on some days covering more than 500 km. Most ospreys return to breed in their third year, often arriving back close to where they were born.

we seem to get more of them in years when rodents are scarce in their north European breeding grounds. The Montagu's harrier is a summer visitor and something of an enigma. With a couple of pairs nesting here in the middle of the 20th century, and only a few sightings recorded since, it is currently confined within the British Isles to the southern half of England. This sporadically seen harrier spends the winter in Africa and is unusual in being almost confined to arable farmland during its stay in England.

The Eurasian eagle owl has the distinction of being the master predator – capable of killing and eating all other birds of prey (including the eagles) found within its mountain or forest breeding range. Since 1996, a pair has bred successfully in northern England, rearing more than twenty young. There have also been one or two nesting pairs in Scotland and a male was recently recorded calling in the north. As this species is regularly kept in captivity, all of these records may be 'escapes'. The snowy owl is an arctic nesting bird, with its nearest breeding grounds in Iceland and the Scandinavian mountains. In 1967 a breeding pair was recorded for the very first time, on Fetlar in Shetland, and in the following five years there was sporadic breeding by the same pair. In 1973 and 1975, two females tried to breed, but the male present could not provision the incubating females, and they deserted their nests. By 1976, the male had gone, and since then several females have been recorded in some years, but with no successful breeding. Birds do over-summer in other parts of Scotland, but we know of no evidence of recent nesting.

In 1995, a male pallid harrier bred with a female hen harrier in Orkney (the eggs were taken by crows); normally, this harrier nests in Eastern Europe and beyond, in Russia and Ukraine, so its presence in Scotland was exceptional. Arguably the most remarkable nesting record is that of a male black kite, observed in April 2005, displaying with a red kite, and nest building a month later (but not breeding). The following year, he returned and paired with a six-year old red kite, producing two flying young – the first ever record of a nesting black kite in Britain and Ireland. Slightly smaller than red kites, and darker in plumage, they breed on a broad front across Europe and on into Asia. That even one of these birds should breed here is exciting, and hints at the sorts of surprises awaiting you in the field.

Buzzards

FACTS

Scientific name:
Buteo buteo

Gaelic: Clamhan

Family:
Accipitridae (hawks,
vultures and eagles)

Measurements:
Body length:
   46-58 cm
Wingspan:
   110-132 cm
Female slightly
larger than male

Population:
15,000-20,000 pairs
in Scotland

Habitat:
Predominantly lowland
farmland, woods and
forests, though breeds
in many upland and
coastal areas

Eggs:
Normally 2-4

Incubation:
36-38 days

For many of us, soaring buzzards are the embodiment of fresh, bright early spring days. Listen to that plaintive, mewing 'peea-ay- peea-ay', uttered by both males and females. Territorial displays typically involve both members of the pair circling together, sometimes interlocking talons and culminating in pursuit dives, the pair bond seemingly reinforced by these intimate moments of soaring on upturned wings. Be aware that at times you may be watching two rival males displaying, often joined by a female or even two. Sometimes, several birds come together to group-soar in ever-rising, encircling parties of ten or more, which finally dissipate into singletons or pairs. Most of these theatrics occur from February onwards, as territories are staked out and nest building begins. In summer, youngsters join the mêlée, with much tumbling and boisterous grasping of talons.

Early in the 19th century buzzards were found across Britain, but by 1900 they were confined to Wales, parts of Scotland and western England, evidently due to persecution. Early in the 20th century their numbers and range recovered, but from 1953 onwards populations crashed due to disease (myxomatosis) in their main prey, rabbits, followed by the effects of pesticide contamination which persisted into the 1960s. Steadily since then numbers have recovered again, with the population spreading eastwards at a rate which accelerated during the 1990s and first decade of the new millennium. The European population, estimated at almost three quarters of a million pairs, is now largely stable, and the British population of possibly as many as sixty thousand pairs is growing steadily, though since 2003 there have been signs of declines in Scotland and Wales.

Buzzards occupy ranges of 2-3 square kilometres, with a section forming a core area which is defended against neighbours. As with most predators, range size varies with food availability, and where rabbits are more plentiful, it is smaller as birds nest closer to one-another – sometimes only 500m apart – whilst in areas of scarce prey abundance, ranges will be much larger. The

Adult buzzards have a contrasting dark band near the tip of the tail.

Buzzards often spend long periods on the ground – feeding on earthworms and invertebrates.

highest densities of buzzards occur in Argyll and southwest and central Scotland, where they take advantage of a varied diet of rabbits, voles, birds and even earthworms. Their large nest may be placed high up in a tree, or on a rocky ledge. Egg laying usually occurs from early April through to early May, lasting 6-9 days, and produces eggs which are white with red, brown or greyish specks. The incubation period lasts 36-38 days, and the young spend 50-60 days in the nest before fledging. Flying young will remain close by the nest for a further four weeks, begging loudly for food from their harassed parents. Immature birds disperse in September, finally settling to breed in their third or fourth year.

Adult buzzards remain on their home range year round, which is unusual compared with the rest of northern Europe, where they are mainly migratory. Males and females are similar in appearance, the male being slightly smaller. In flight they appear short-winged and compact, with quick wing beats, and sometimes they hover whilst hunting or even hang in the air. There is much variation in plumage – some appear very dark, most brownish and a few a creamy white. Juveniles are distinguished from adults by their paler eyes, faint, narrow tail bars and teardrop-like streaks on their underparts revealing whitish background feathers. Adults have dark brown eyes, broad and dark tail bands (appearing from below as a blackish tail fringe), and a distinctive pale crescent across the breast. They are much underrated as the beginner's bird of prey!

FACTS

Young fledge:
50-60 days

Of interest:
The buzzard has overtaken the kestrel to become our most abundant bird of prey. The scientific name *Buteo* aptly refers to buzzards being 'broad winged and soaring'. The word buzzard derives from the old French *buisart* 'inferior hawk', from the Latin *buteonem*, a kind of hawk, perhaps with the *-art* suffix being used dismissively.

Golden Eagles

In a remote Highland glen, late in winter as an icy snowstorm makes way for shafts of sunlight, you may see these imperious birds displaying. Soaring first, shortly the male plummets towards his mate, and she tumble-rolls, striking out with her massive talons, as he seems to get too close. These rollicking displays, with their looping and plummeting dives, are heart warming and thrilling. You may even hear the wind gusting through the tail and broad wing feathers, though most of these antics are performed high up, over ridges, and well out of earshot. What a spectacle!

Nest building begins in the autumn, with fresh tree branches or large heather sticks being added to the eyrie. These may be decades old, some handed down through generations. Some nests are several metres tall and wide, appearing like sacks of coal piled two or three high, but others can be quite straggly, so much so that in a very few, eggs or chicks tumble out. Most pairs have alternate eyries within their territory, sometimes several kilometres apart; they may build up one or more sites each year before choosing one in which to nest. From mid March through to early April, generally two eggs are laid over 3-6 days, and these hatch after being incubated by both birds for around 44 days. During this period little may be seen of the eagles, one sitting tightly and not budging even when the nest is deeply covered by snow, and the other hunting several miles away and making just one or two visits in the day.

The oval, dull white and lightly marked eggs hatch a few days apart. Then begins the struggle of 'Cain and Abel', with the elder chick bullying the younger, which will only survive if food is sufficient for both – and in some regions twins rarely make it to fledgling. The chicks are in the nest for about 80 days, from late April through to mid September, becoming noisy and seemingly abandoned by their parents towards their final days in the now worn looking, flattened nest with all manner of prey remains scattered around and below.

A young bird reaching its first winter has large white central wing

The golden eagle was voted Scotland's national bird in a major newspaper poll.

The oldest ringed golden eagle in Scotland was one that reached 16 years – half that reached by a Swedish bird, aged 32.

patches, and a white tail fringed black; older birds lose the white above and below on each wing, though even into their fourth and fifth years they have white or pale tails and pale panels on the upper wing. The adult, from five years onwards, is almost uniformly dark brown, with a golden crown and hind neck.

Eagles feed mainly on rabbits, hares and grouse as well as sheep and deer carrion, but take from a wide spectrum of bird and mammal prey, including other raptors such as young hen harriers, buzzards and peregrine. The 440 or so territories, varying in size from about 9 to 75 square kilometres, are distributed across the Scottish Highlands and Islands, with no more than a handful south of there. Golden eagles breed at higher densities in parts of the west (such as

Harris, Skye and Mull) yet more successfully in the east, where live prey is more plentiful. Sadly, eagles are still illegally killed on some eastern grouse-moors, and if the climate continues to get wetter in the west there are concerns that the population as a whole may shift from current stability to decline, especially if more of the western territories fail to produce fledged young.

In Ireland, the golden eagle reintroduction project released 53 birds in Donegal during 2001-2008. Chicks were collected from nests in Scotland and reared in captivity, without human contact, for a further 5-7 weeks before being released. By 2009 there had been two successful breeding attempts, with five territories holding adult or sub-adult pairs, and another three with single birds.

FACTS

Eggs: 2 (sometimes 1, occasionally 3)

Incubation: 41-45 days

Young fledge: 72-86 days; often only the first hatched chick survives

Of interest: The scientific name *chrysaetos* comes from the Greek word for gold, *khrusos*, referring to the head and neck. Some adults may breed for ten or many years more, and tend to stay together until one partner dies.

Hen Harriers

FACTS

Scientific name:
Circus cyaneus

Gaelic:
Clamhan-nan-cearc

Family:
Accipitridae (hawks, vultures and eagles)

Measurements:
Body length:
45-55 cm
Wingspan:
97-118 cm
Female larger than male

Population:
630 breeding
pairs in 2004

Habitat:
Nests in heather moorland, wet heaths and bogs, and young forestry. Hunts mainly on rough grassland

Eggs: 4-6

Incubation: 30 days

A bird of open country throughout the year, the hen harrier is *par excellence* the raptor of rolling heather moorland. Sadly, this latter association has greatly affected the birds' fortunes over the past 200 years. Harriers were once abundant throughout the mires, bogs, moors and 'wastes' of Scotland. Loss of habitat through land drainage and agricultural improvement together with the rising popularity of game shooting led to a widespread decline. Quickly exterminated throughout the Scottish mainland, by the end of the 19th century, hen harriers were found only in Orkney and the Hebrides. From these island strongholds, populations increased briefly during the two World Wars, but with birds losing ground in some areas after the Second War. From the early 1950s harriers were able to establish a foothold in the young conifer forests, which were increasingly being planted – with many on former grouse moors. Protected by forest rangers, who viewed harriers as beneficial in reducing rodent abundance, the number of breeding pairs increased rapidly.

The population probably reached a peak in the 1960s and 1970s, but as these forests matured, many ground-nesting hen harriers spread back to the open moor, where their fortunes have been mixed. Today sadly, many hen harriers attempting to breed on grouse moors fail. Nesting hen harriers are now found primarily in the southwest, throughout Argyll, the Inner and Outer Hebrides, the far north in Sutherland and Caithness and on Orkney. The most recent survey in 2004 estimated there were 630 breeding pairs in Scotland.

Harriers hunt by quartering low over open ground and aided by long legs and sharp talons, drop quickly on potential prey – a vole, young rabbit or small bird. They are unusual amongst birds of prey because of the striking differences in size and appearance between the sexes. This is largely due to their different roles during the breeding season. The larger female alone carries out the incubation of eggs and brooding and feeding of young. She is a cryptic brown above and streaked off-white below, with a long barred tail and striking white rump.

Male hen harriers do not acquire their striking plumage until their second year.

Early naturalists thought 'ring-tailed' harriers (female hen harriers) were a separate species from grey adult males.

The male, ghostly grey above, unblemished white below and with black wing tips, engages in a spectacular aerial display at the start of the breeding season. The so-called 'sky dance' involves the male circling high over the breeding grounds before plummeting earthwards, only to sweep upwards at the last moment, roll over on his back at the top of the climb before diving to earth again. This sequence will be repeated dozens of times and the display can last up to 15 minutes at a time. The nest, made from heather stems and dried grass, is concealed on the ground in deep heather, in rushes or at the base of a young tree in an upland plantation. Four to six white eggs are laid during late April and in May and hatch after 30 days of incubation.

The female tends the young whilst the male does all the hunting, dropping the prey, which is caught by the female in a spectacular aerial food pass. Male chicks fledge after 28 days; females at 32 but both remain dependant on their parents for food for another four weeks.

Most hen harriers leave their natal moors in the early autumn, moving south to lowland farmland and coastal marshes. Some birds, mainly males, cross to the Continent reaching France and Spain for the winter. At this time of year they roost communally in reed beds, marshes or on heaths. With up to a dozen or so harriers milling over the roosting site as darkness falls, this is one of Scotland's finest but increasingly rare wildlife spectacles.

FACTS

Young fledge:
28-32 days, but depend on parents for food for another four weeks

Of interest:
The origins of the name 'harrier' are uncertain, but may come from the medieval English *hayrer* (small hunting dog) and French *errier* (wanderer), or may be associated with hunting hares. The scientific name *Circus* may come from the Greek word for a ring, *kirkos*, referring to the female's ringtail.

FACTS

Scientific name:
Pandion haliaetus

Gaelic:
Iolaire-iasgaich

Family:
Panionidae (osprey)

Measurements:
Body length:
  52-60 cm
Wingspan:
  152-167 cm
Female is five to
ten percent larger
than the male

Population:
About 200 pairs,
increasing slowly

Ospreys

Back in 1954, all of this was inconceivable. In that year a pair of ospreys bred at Loch Garten – the first recorded nesting in Britain since 1916. Enmeshed in secrecy, with round-the-clock guards posted near the nest, and all sorts of whodunit stories about earlier nesting attempts thwarted by egg collectors, the return of the osprey came at a time of burgeoning environmental awareness. In that same year, a piece of landmark legislation, the Protection of Birds Act, made egg collecting illegal. We will never know if ospreys bred in Scotland from the 1920s to the early 1950s; we suspect they did, with several sightings of adults each summer. But since the mid 1950s the population grew steadily, to as many as 210 pairs in 2008. A combination of nest protection measures and provision of artificial nest platforms made this great recovery possible – despite the efforts of egg-thieves, who as recently as 1989 plundered a quarter of active nests. Osprey chicks from Scotland have also been translocated to central England, where a small breeding population has been established, and has even spilled over into North Wales.

Each year the birds return to breeding areas from late-March, males tending to arrive first. When his mate returns, the male may sky dance excitedly and intensely close to their huge eyrie. Males can be distinguished from females as they are slightly smaller, whiter below with less marked breast bands (and experienced observers can recognise individual birds by subtle variations in feather patterning). Most ospreys breed for the first time at three years old and fidelity to both the nest site and mate is thought to be strong. Those surviving to breeding age live for an average of eight years – the record being 32 years.

Built on the top of a tree, or possibly an electricity pylon, some nests have been used for decades – the Loch Garten site has been occupied for more than 50 years with three

When diving for fish, ospreys are often completely submerged.

Ospreys are unique amongst Scottish raptors – feeding solely on fish.

different nests used. Nest sites tend to be in open woods and usually within 10 kilometres of lochs, rivers or estuaries well fished by the adults. Egg laying takes place from mid April, with older and more experienced pairs nesting earliest, and in turn being the most successful. Typically three eggs are laid, which are oval, slightly glossy and have a creamy white background richly marked with red-brown blotches and spots. Incubation starts with the first egg, lasts 34-43 days, and is undertaken by both sexes. Whilst the female does the greater share of this work (and always takes the night shift), the male provides courtship feeds of fish – eating the front part himself and delivering the rest to the female, sometimes before he takes a turn at incubation duties.

The chicks hatch asynchronously and, while the female broods them, the male works hard to provision the family, bringing an average of five fish per day, and more as the chicks grow. The young are tended closely by the female for the first ten days, and fledge at 40-59 days. Towards the end of fledging period, the female may quit the nesting area, leaving the male to feed the flying youngsters. From late August through to late September juveniles disperse and begin their first 3,000 mile migration to winter quarters in west Africa.

So, if you have the good fortune to see an osprey plunge, wings kinked and talons outstretched, and pluck a fish from just below the water surface, muse on the remarkable success of this bird. The development of the nature conservation movement in Britain is closely linked with the return of this bird – which fired the imagination of people wanting a better future for wildlife.

FACTS

Habitat:
Breeds in lowland woods by lochs, rivers and the coast, though can travel many miles from where it is fishes; tends to nest at the top of pine trees

Eggs:
2-4 (normally 3)

Incubation:
34-43 days

Young fledge:
40-59 days

Of interest: In recent years, some of our ospreys have been satellite-tracked to their African wintering grounds, with websites reporting their migratory travails.

Peregrine Falcons

FACTS

Scientific name:
Falco peregrinus

Gaelic:
Seabhag-ghorm

Family:
Falconidae
(falcons and allies)

Measurements:
Body length:
   38-45 cm (male);
   46-51 (female)
Wingspan:
   89-100 cm (male);
   104-113 cm (female)

Population:
544 breeding pairs
in Scotland

Habitat:
Found breeding across
the world's land and
coast, from tundra to
tropics, and absent
only from the polar
extremes. Now often
seen and heard in
our towns and cities.

Eggs: 3 or 4

Thrilling and dramatic, peregrines on the hunt offer the *piece de resistance*. Watch the tiercel (the male falcon) vigilant from a rocky vantage or whilst circling high: he spots something on the wing, flies in pursuit, then rises before stooping with wings folded and held back; now plunging at breakneck speed he strikes the head or neck with his talons, occasionally accompanied by a loud 'whack', as the victim dissipates into a cloud of feathers; and finally up he loops, and then down again to retrieve his quarry by now tumbling — fluttering even — before being torn up and devoured. What a predator, with as many as 50 different bird species taken in some regions, ranging in size from siskins, chaffinches and skylarks to mallard, grouse and great black-backed gull.

For a bird so powerful and grand, and the female (sometimes called 'the falcon') is fifteen percent larger than the male, the nest is understated — a scrape on a cliff ledge about 20 cm in diameter and 3-5 cm deep, or in an old nest of a raven, or even an eagle, buzzard or heron. But the crags can be massive and sheer, with the largest ones chosen for nesting in. Courtship displays begin in early March, with the tiercel — but sometimes the female — performing figure of eights, switchback swoops and looping-the-loop aerobatics. Together, the pair will high circle and flight play. Flying across the crag, they can be noisy, raucous even, as the 'rhek-rhek-rhek' cries shatter the silence of the moment. Three or four eggs are laid at 2-day intervals from early April onwards, with coastal and lowland birds nesting earliest. The eggs are oval, buff and heavily marked with red and red-brown markings; such is their beauty that collectors robbed many clutches, and some continue with this illegal activity.

Incubation, mainly by the female (and always by her at night) lasts 28-35 days, with the first and last chicks hatching no more than two days apart. At first snowy white, the chicks are tended closely by the female whilst the tiercel provisions her. After about 10 days she hunts as well, close to the nest, with the growing chicks receiving 4-11 feeding visits each day, mainly around dawn and in the evening. The youngsters fledge at

The male peregrine is the 'tiercel', and the female is the 'falcon'.

5-6 weeks, with the smaller ones (males) flying first. Both parents continue to feed the young, which disperse from their natal territories during August-September onwards.

In appearance the adults are distinctive with their slate-grey upperparts, barred and spotted white breast and belly, and black head with a distinctive moustache. Juveniles are dark brown above with pale streaks on the nape and behind the eyes, and heavily streaked (not barred) below. Most peregrines will not breed until their second year, with some youngsters travelling far in their first year. In Britain the adults tend to stay on their home ranges year round, though less productive ones may be abandoned in winter.

This pugnacious predator was a *cause celebre* of environmental change. In the 1950s-1960s numbers declined worldwide due to pesticides in the food chain working their way up to cause peregrines to lay thin-shelled eggs that were prone to breakages. As a result of painstaking research and lobbying, the main pesticide culprit, DDT, was banned in the US in 1972 and in the European Union in 1986. Monitoring of peregrines continues, with five national surveys undertaken so far, the most recent giving an estimate of 544 breeding pairs in Scotland.

The origins of the word peregrine are obscure, but probably derived from the Latin *peregrinus*, meaning foreign or abroad, or the Latin verb *peregrinari*, to travel. Oddly, you might have expected a derivation associated with its prowess as arch predator, but then again it might refer to birds being brought in from abroad, as prized falconers' birds.

And finally, a curiosity, for Scotland's large birds of prey have many places named after them – Creag na h'Iolaire (eagle crag), Creag an Fhithich (raven crag) and Eun or Eoin

For acceleration in level flight, no bird can match the peregrine.

(eagle or osprey place) – but only a couple are named Creag an t'Seabhaig (Falcon Crag). The foremost expert on the peregrine, the late Derek Ratcliffe, hinted at the reason for this in his classic monograph on the peregrine – in medieval days the nesting places of the prized peregrine would have been so jealously guarded that country folk would have been discouraged from drawing attention to them! And now we have peregrines nesting in some of our cities.

FACTS

Incubation:
28-35 days

Young fledge:
Fledge at 5-6 weeks, with the smaller ones (males) flying first

Of interest: Falconry was practiced as far back as 2000 BC in ancient Egypt and China.

Red Kites

FACTS

Scientific name:
Milvus milvus

Gaelic:
Clamhan-gobhlach

Family:
Accipitridae (hawks,
vultures and eagles)

Measurements:
Body length:
  61-72 cm
Wingspan:
  140-165 cm

The red kite is Scotland's most handsome bird of prey and one of the easiest to recognise due to its large size, richly coloured plumage and long forked tail. Essentially scavengers, they are most likely to be seen in the air searching for dead birds and animals on which to feed. They also eat invertebrates such as beetles and earthworms and even snatch meat scraps from gardens. They were once widespread throughout mainland Britain, but their extermination during the 19th century is a sad example from that era of intolerance that led to the destruction of many hapless predatory species, collectively labelled as 'vermin'. By the end of that century, kites were extinct in Scotland and England and only a handful of pairs survived in remote valleys of central Wales. In 1989, reintroduction schemes were started in the Chilterns of southern England (they were seen again in London, after a lengthy absence, in January 2006) and on the Black Isle in the Scottish Highlands, leading to the re-establishment of two new populations. Scottish kite numbers were augmented with additional reintroductions near Stirling (1996), Dumfries & Galloway (2000) and Aberdeen (2007). The breeding population had reached 150 pairs by 2009 and should increase further.

In profile, the adult kite is rich chestnut in colour, with a whitish/grey head and striking lemon-yellow eyes. The sexes are similar – the female being slightly larger. In their first year, young kites are more buff coloured, with a less contrasting head and a brownish eye. The legs are relatively short for a bird of prey giving the bird an ungainly appearance when on the ground. But in the air, it is masterful – the iconic buoyant and graceful dancer.

A past name for the red kite was the 'salmon-tailed gled'.

Along with its large angular wings, which have contrasting white panels and prominent blackish 'fingers', the soaring kite spreads its long rufous-red tail as a fan, and twists it rudder-like to give surprising manoeuvrability.

Adults are resident and remain close to their nest site throughout the year. They commence breeding when two or three years old and enjoy long lives if not molested, some birds reaching 15-20 or more years. Scottish kites mate for life and lay three eggs, sometimes four, in early April. The large untidy stick nest, lined with sheep wool and adorned with rubbish such as rags, newspapers and polythene bags, is built high in a tree, usually near a woodland edge or in an isolated copse. The eggs are a dirty white in colour and incubation, mainly by the female, lasts about 32 days. The male provides food for the family during the first few weeks but as the chicks grow, the female assists in foraging; more live prey and less carrion may feature in the diet at this time. Small rabbits, and young rooks and crows appear particularly important, their remains found in most nests examined. The young fledge at 7 weeks and spend another 4-6 weeks near their nest site before reaching independence. Prior to maturity, young kites may undertake long dispersal movements, often not returning for a year or two. A few of the recorded movements of ringed Scottish born kites have been remarkable. Single birds have reached Spain and Portugal; another was photographed in the Azores in mid Atlantic, and yet another was found alive in Iceland.

Red kites form large communal roosts

Broods of 2 or 3 are most frequent amongst Scottish red kites.

in secluded woodland during the winter months. These can regularly hold 30-50 birds, the largest in Scotland often holding over 70. The same roost locations will be used each night, sometimes over many years. Kites will also congregate where there is an abundance of carrion, such as a deer carcass or an unburied farm animal. For this reason they are easily attracted to kite feeding stations with scraps of meat provided on a daily basis. Feeding stations offer the exciting spectacle of large numbers of foraging red kites from the shelter of a visitor hide or centre. The opportunity to marvel at the aerial agility and prowess of these birds should not be missed.

Regrettably, there are still those who view kites with ignorance and suspicion. Each year several are found dead – shot or killed with illegal poison baits – slowing the recovery of the Scottish population. Despite this, the future of red kites is looking increasingly secure and the species is destined to become ever more familiar over Scottish skies.

FACTS

The female is slightly larger than the male

Population: 150 pairs by 2009, and growing as the reintroduction programmes take effect

Habitat:
Rural, open fields associated with woods

Eggs: 2 or 3, sometimes 4

Incubation: 32 days

Young fledge:
49 days, but spend up to another 6 weeks near the nest before becoming independent

Of interest:
Red kites were once so plentiful that Shakespeare described London as a 'city of red kites & crows'. The first toy kite took its name from this bird, in 1664.

Scientific name:
Haliaeetus albicilla

Gaelic: Iolaire-mhara;
Iolaire sùil na grèine,
eagle of the sunlit eye

Family:
Accipitridae (hawks,
vultures and eagles)

Measurements:
Body length:
  76-92 cm
Wingspan:
  190-240 cm
The female is up to
a quarter heavier and
well over ten percent
larger than the male

Population:
46 breeding pairs
in 2009

Habitat: Breeds along
the sea coast, and by
large sea lochs where
it is associated with
upland and woodland
terrain, though formerly
occupied lowland areas

Sea Eagles

Massive and vulture-like, with a heavy beak and long neck, the return of this, our largest bird of prey, is cause for special celebration. If you have to name one bird which has recently benefited from human actions in Scotland, this is it.

Of all birds of prey in Europe this is the bird which has increased, or at least recovered, the most in recent decades. Across Europe, sea eagles declined from the early 19th century because of persecution and pollution. Here in Britain, the species became extinct in 1918 (the last pair bred on Skye in 1916), following decades of intense human persecution.

Reintroduction of sea eagles to Scotland began in 1975 using nestlings from Norway. The first eggs were laid in the wild in 1983, with flying young produced two years later.

By 2009 there were 46 breeding pairs (producing 36 flying young) in the Hebrides and in the west and north Highlands.

In 2007, a five-year release programme began in Fife, to try and re-establish the species in the east of Scotland. In August 2009 the third batch of Norwegian sea eagles was released in Fife. Fifteen birds were brought here, following the release of 30 eagles over the previous two years. This is the third phase of an ambitious reintroduction programme. The return of sea eagles to Mull, Skye and other parts of western Scotland has been one of the most outstanding conservation success stories of recent times.

The reintroduction of these birds is not without controversy, and there remain concerns amongst some farmers and others about their impacts on lambs and other livestock. Sea eagles do indeed take lambs, though many of these are dead already when taken. Their main prey is fish, seabirds, waterbirds, rabbits and carrion.

Occupying their breeding ranges year round, the pair begins its courting, circling and looping displays in January, not much more than 100 metres above a crag, and often in windy conditions. What a sight, as these massive birds with their long, broad wings tumble and roll, flight-play and talon-touch. Scottish birds tend to be quiet,

In the west Highlands, sea-eagles frequently scavenge near inshore fishing boats.

Described as a 'flying barn-door', the sea-eagle has a broader wing-span than golden eagles and a more massive beak.

but in the Baltic countries the displaying pair may duet loudly.

The large nests in trees or on cliff ledges are made from branches, heather and seaweed, and lined with grass, moss and lichens. Sea eagles are not known to nest on the ground in Scotland, but do so in Norway and Iceland. Two, sometimes three eggs are laid, from late February through to mid April, hatching after 38 days. The female takes the greater share of incubation duties (especially at night) with the pair changing shifts every 3-4 hours during the day.

From the broad oval, dull white eggs the chicks hatch several days apart. For the first two to three weeks the eaglets are brooded closely, mainly by the female whilst the male hunts. The young fledge at between 70 and 84 days, remaining close to the nest and still dependent on the parents for a further month or more. They begin to disperse from their natal site in September, although some may remain nearby for much of the winter. They will not breed for many years, some nesting for the first time at three years old, but others not until seven or more years. Interestingly, Scottish birds breed for the first time earlier than those in Norway and Sweden, something that may be common in re-introduced birds.

The adults and juveniles are easily told apart, the latter darker and richer brown, with most of the tail dark (though pale when viewed against a strong light) and the trailing edge of the wings appearing to bulge in the middle.

FACTS

Eggs: 2, sometimes 3

Incubation: 38 days

Young fledge: 70-84 days, but dependant on the parents for several more months

Of interest: Arguably belonging to one of the most ancient of all groups of birds in the world, the sea eagle has featured strongly in prehistory. In Orkney, there are Pictish stone carvings of the bird, and their bones have been found in 4000 year old burial mounds.

FACTS

Scientific name:
Tyto alba

Gaelic: Comhachag-bhàn

Family: Tytonidae
(barn owls and allies)

Measurements:
Body length:
  33-39 cm
Wingspan:
  80-95 cm
Male normally
paler than female

Population:
500-1,000 pairs

Habitat: Farmland with
scattered copses, old
buildings and grassy or
rushy fields. Sometimes
nests in villages, usually
in old buildings

Eggs: 2-9 eggs,
sometimes up to 12 eggs

Incubation:
Begins with the first egg
and lasts for 29-34 days;
most eggs hatching after
30-32 days

Barn Owls

The ghostly whiteness of this bird strikes you first, as it flits low and silent over unkempt fields at dusk, wavering over a ditch or grassy bank. Largely nocturnal, its scientific name, *Tyto alba*, describes it aptly as a white (from the Latin, *albus*) owl (the Greek, *tuto*).

This totemic farmland bird has undergone long-term declines in Britain during the 20th century due to persecution, intensification of farming and loss of nesting and feeding habitats. Such was the concern for barn owls that by the early 1990s substantial effort was put into releasing captive bred birds; 2,000 plus were released annually in Britain, and around 25,000 nest boxes were provided. Gradually, there has been some recovery, especially in areas where suitable nest sites in derelict buildings or trees are absent.

In Scotland, barn owls are at the edge of their range: the small, scattered populations nesting west of Aberdeen, around Inverness, into Easter Ross and now as far north as Sutherland and Caithness are the most northerly in the world! They are susceptible to hard winters and cannot survive in areas with extended snow cover (more than about 15 days in the year), hence the bulk of the Scottish population occurs in the low-lying areas of the south and west and they are absent from the Western and Northern Isles. Nevertheless, the Scottish population has increased recently. Just over 400 pairs were recorded in 2007 and there may be as many as 1,000 – though the harsh winter of 2009-10 may set them back.

The sexes are similar in size but readily told apart if seen clearly. The male has pure white underparts, with white extending up the sides of his neck and into the face, whereas the female has a wash of light ochre on the breast and belly with distinctive black flecking. And look at that head – a white, heart-shaped 'face' with dark eyes set against the mottled light grey, golden and buff upperparts. At the start of the nesting phase the male utters loud, hissing 'shrrreee' screams, typically just after dusk. He may take off on in pursuit of the female or on a display flight around his territory, calling repeatedly. The name, barn owl, reflects a penchant for nesting in farm buildings, especially where

A once popular name for the barn owl was the white owl.

there may be a dearth of natural sites in tree-hollows or rock cavities. The nest is no more than a scrape amongst a pile of regurgitated pellets in which between two and nine pure white eggs are laid, at two to three day intervals, though as far apart as seven days if feeding conditions are poor. The eggs are light in weight compared with those of other cavity dwelling owls, possibly an adaption for laying large clutches when food is plentiful. With incubation beginning on the first egg, and lasting 29-34 days, the size differences between chicks can be great. The female alone incubates, fed by her mate from the start of egg-laying until long after the chicks have hatched, as many as 16 times each night.

As the chicks develop, they are brooded by the female until the youngest is 12-16 days old. Size differences between siblings become evident quickly, with some double the size of others. The young can fly at 50-55 days, but need a further 20 days for their feathers to develop fully. Fed by both parents towards the end of the nestling period, it is at this time that the wheezy, snoring begging calls of the young can be heard.

For birds with such enchanting eyes, it may come as a surprise to learn that prey is located mainly by sound, and often in pitch-blackness. Hunting from perches or from flight, the heart-shaped face channels sound waves, enabling acutely accurate detection of the location and movements of prey. Feeding mainly on voles, barn owls prefer to hunt along woodland edges, fences, ditches and even roadsides, where prey are most abundant. Roads are, however, dangerous places, responsible for about 60% of deaths in Scottish owls (based on recoveries of the corpses of ringed birds). Field voles go

Males are pure white below and lack the female's black flecking.

through three year 'boom and bust' cycles in numbers, and tracking these ups and downs, year on year, there can be three-to five fold differences in barn owl numbers, with the low years due in large part to poor survival of chicks (up to 45% dying in the nest) and winter starvation when prey numbers are low.

Utterly compelling, with long, soft wings producing that silent wafting flight, and dangling feet when hovering, this is the most beautiful of the owls.

FACTS

Young fledge: 50-55 days, but flight feathers not fully developed until 70-75 days

Of interest: It's nicknames of ghost owl, hobgoblin owl, screech owl, demon owl and death owl betray old associations with bad omens in rural districts.

Scotland

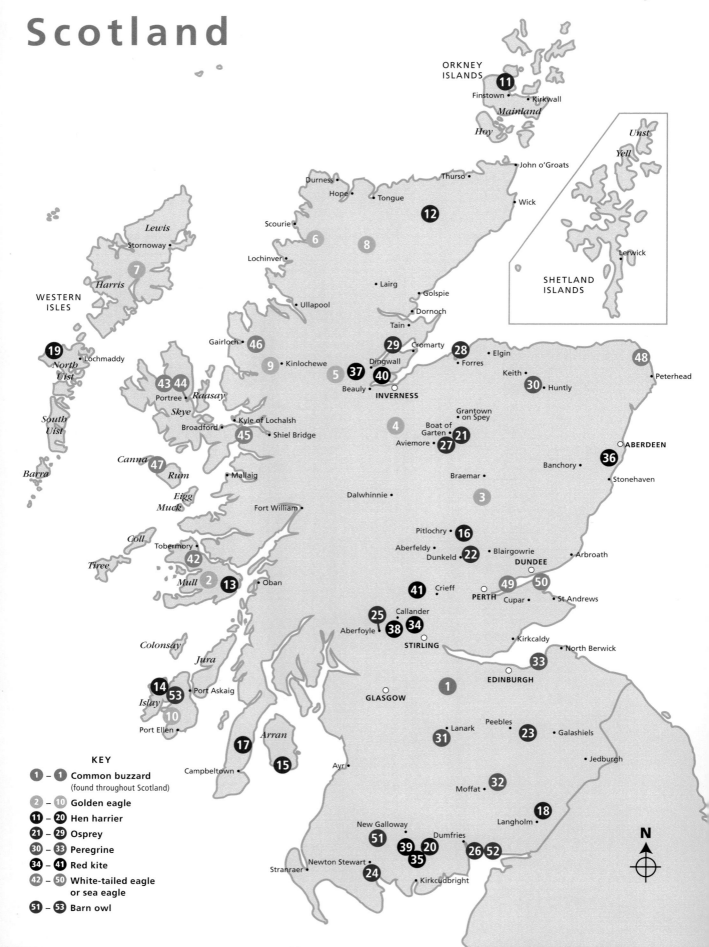

ORKNEY ISLANDS
Finstown • ⑪ • Kirkwall
Mainland
Hoy

Unst
Yell
SHETLAND ISLANDS
• Lerwick

Lewis
Stornoway •

Harris
WESTERN ISLES
⑦

⑲
North Uist
• Lochmaddy

South Uist

Barra

Durness •
Hope •
Scourie •
Lochinver •
⑥
⑧
• Tongue
Thurso •
• John o'Groats
⑫
• Wick

• Lairg
• Golspie
• Ullapool
• Dornoch
Tain •

Gairloch •
⑨
⑤
⑰
• Kinlochewe
Dingwall
⑳
⑩
Beauly •
INVERNESS
• Cromarty
⑳
⑭
Elgin •
Forres •
⑳
Keith •
⑩ • Huntly
⑱
• Peterhead

⑭
⑭
Portree •
Raasay
Skye
Broadford •
• Kyle of Lochalsh
⑮
• Shiel Bridge

⑭
④
• Grantown on Spey
Boat of Garten •
⑳
Aviemore •
⑳
Banchory •
⑳ **ABERDEEN**
• Stonehaven

Canna
⑰
Rum
Eigg
Muck
• Mallaig

Braemar •
③
Dalwhinnie •

Fort William •

Coll
Tobermory •
⑭
Tiree
Mull
②
⑬
• Oban

Pitlochry • ⑯
Aberfeldy •
Dunkeld •
⑳ • Blairgowrie
DUNDEE
• Arbroath

④
• Crieff
⑭
⑳
PERTH
• Cupar
• St Andrews

Colonsay
Jura

⑳
Callander •
⑳ ⑭
Aberfoyle •
STIRLING
• Kirkcaldy
⑳
⑳
• North Berwick

⑭
⑤
Islay
• Port Askaig
⑩
Port Ellen •

Arran
⑰
⑮
Campbeltown •

GLASGOW
①
EDINBURGH

• Lanark
⑳
Peebles •
⑳ • Galashiels
Ayr •
⑳
Moffat •
• Jedburgh

⑱
Langholm •

New Galloway •
⑤
⑳ ⑳
Dumfries •
⑳ ⑳
⑳
Newton Stewart •
Stranraer •
⑳
• Kirkcudbright

N

KEY

① – ① **Common buzzard** (found throughout Scotland)

② – ⑩ **Golden eagle**

⑪ – ⑳ **Hen harrier**

㉑ – ㉙ **Osprey**

㉚ – ㉝ **Peregrine**

㉞ – ㊶ **Red kite**

㊷ – ㊿ **White-tailed eagle or sea eagle**

㊿ – ⑤ **Barn owl**

Places to see Birds of Prey

Watching birds is a pastime enjoyed by millions of people in Britain. Please keep a respectful distance so that disturbance is kept to a minimum. In Scotland, there are thousands of places where you can watch birds of prey, and often the real excitement comes from discovering these places for yourself. We have drawn together a list of places where you have a good chance of seeing some of these birds of prey. Several organisations provide excellent information, notably the Scottish Raptor Study Groups (www.scottishraptorgroups.org), Scottish Natural Heritage, with details of what should be seen on National Nature Reserves (www.nnr-scotland.org.uk), the Royal Society for the Protection of Birds (www.rspb.org.uk/scotland), the Scottish Wildlife Trust (www.swt.org.uk) and the Forestry Commission (www.forestry.gov.uk/scotland). Visit Scotland provides up to date information on some activities (www.visitscotland.com).

COMMON BUZZARD

1 Probably the first large bird of prey a visitor will encounter in Scotland and often seen soaring close to roads on fine days. Sometimes mistaken for an eagle, but the latter much larger birds will not be seen until you reach the more remote Highland glens or the Western Isles – and its buzzards, not eagles, that sometimes hover! Buzzards perch freely on fence posts, power poles, and in trees. Close views can be had at the four red kite feeding stations and on all the various trails and locations given for all other species listed.

GOLDEN EAGLE

2 For eagle enthusiasts, a visit to the Island of Mull in Argyll can be very rewarding but some effort must be made to obtain good views. The island holds good numbers of both species and whilst there is a public viewing hide for white-tailed eagles, those seeking golden must be prepared to take to the hills. Alternatively, take a day trip with one of the several wildlife tour operators that are based on the island. The website gives details of these operators and also gives details of recent sightings of eagles and other birds.
www.mullbirds.com

3 The A93 running south of Braemar in Aberdeenshire to the Glenshee Ski Centre is one of the classic routes to search for soaring eagles above the surrounding hills, particularly the higher sections of the road. Indeed, in many parts of the Cairngorms you have a chance to see golden eagles in mountain and ancient forest habitats.

4 The upper reaches of the River Findhorn near Coignafearn in Inverness-shire (NH 712181) are also classic Golden Eagle country. The area is reached by following the river upstream for nine miles along an unclassified road starting just before the old Findhorn Bridge, two miles south of Tomatin. Tomatin lies just off the A9, 15 miles south of Inverness. Large herds of red deer graze the hills and there is a chance of seeing other raptors such as buzzard, merlin and peregrine.

5 To the west of Inverness lies the lovely Strathconon. Take the A832 from the Tore roundabout on the A9 north of Inverness to the village of Marybank (NH480537). Where the main road turns sharp right, follow a minor road straight on for a further 20 miles to the head of the glen at Loch Beannacharain. Make frequent stops along the way, there are ample pull-ins, to view the skyline and hilltops for eagles and other birds of prey such as red kites, buzzards and peregrines.

6 For the adventurous, a boat trip along Loch Glencoul in northwest Sutherland offers the opportunity of seeing both white-tailed and golden eagle against some of the most impressive and awe-inspiring scenery in Scotland. Boat trips operate twice daily from May to September, departing from Kylesku jetty (NC230338) just off the A894 Ledmore to Scourie road and just to the south of the Kylesku Bridge. Telephone 01971 502345 for sailing information.

7 The Western Isles hold some of the highest golden eagle densities and a drive around the islands of Lewis & Harris under favourable weather conditions will not fail to provide sightings, particularly the A859 linking Lewis with North Harris. The islands can be reached by regular ferry sailings from Ullapool.

8 The single-track roads in northwest Sutherland offer breathtaking views and special opportunities to see golden eagles. If you go to Altnaharra, taking the A836 north of Lairg, and then follow the winding Hope road northwest, you have a good chance of seeing them. Carry on when you get to Hope, driving west on the A838 to Durness and then south to Laxford Bridge, and you should see more eagles and other raptors.

9 A visit to the Beinn Eighe NNR offers great opportunities to see golden eagles. From the Tore roundabout on the A9, take the A835. After Garve, leave on the A832 for Achnasheen and Kinlochewe where there is a visitor centre: www.nnr-scotland.org.uk/reserve. Go west to Gairloch, or north to Ullapool and beyond to Lochinver, and you have a good chance of seeing eagles against a backdrop of magnificent Highland scenery. Treat yourself to a walk at the Knockan Centre and to the Bone Caves, south of Inchnadamph, and you may have great sightings of eagles. Details at: www.knockan-crag.co.uk

10 The Isle of Islay holds an important population of golden eagles sometimes visible from the islands roads. Visit the web site and click on Islay birds for details. www.isle-of-islay.net

HEN HARRIER

The Scottish islands are the best places to see hen harriers. On the mainland an element of luck and patient watching is required.

11 The hen harriers on Orkney have been studied longer than any other bird of prey species and the RSPB Birsay Moors reserve (map reference HY340240) is one of the best places to see them. Details at www.rspb.org.uk/ reserves/guide/b/birsaymoors/about.asp

12 Another RSPB reserve, this time at Forsinard Flows in Highland (NC891425) has breeding hen harriers as well as a visitor centre and other moorland species. Treat yourself and take the train north of Inverness to Forsinard, and enjoy the walks available. The visitor centre is situated on the train station platform. Details at www.rspb.co.uk/reserves/guide/ f/forsinard/about.asp

13 Throughout the year, the island of Mull is a raptor hot spot. Hen harriers are one of the island specialities. They can occur virtually anywhere. For details visit www.explore-isle-of-mull.co.uk/birds-of-prey.htm

14 On Islay, the RSPB reserve at Loch Gruinart is an excellent venue for seeing hen harriers throughout the year along with many other exciting species. Visit their web site at www.rspb.org.uk/reserves/guide/l/lochgruin art/about.asp For information about hen harriers and other species on Islay visit www.isle-of-islay.net

15 Visit Kilmory on the Isle of Arran during the summer where Forestry Commission Scotland will set up an annual CCTV viewing facility at a hen harriers nest. Details at *www.forestry. gov.uk/arranhenharriers*

16 The A924, Pitlochry to Blairgowrie road, about 4 miles from the centre of Pitlochry, at approximately map reference NN978605 is worth a visit. Park safely along the moorland section of this road and scan the surrounding countryside for hunting birds.

17 In the spring and summer, hen harriers occur in good numbers throughout the Argyll peninsula. Try walking some of the young forestry and moorland sections of the Kintyre Way. *www.kintyreway.com*

18 At Langholm, Dumfries-shire, there are superb opportunities to see displaying harriers from the road. Taking the A7 south, and just before you enter Langholm, turn left and take the small (unclassified) road up, by the tall Monument. Drive on about half a mile and park in one of the few large passing places, and look out for hen harriers against an attractive moorland backdrop. You may see merlins and peregrines as well. This is part of the Langholm Moor Demonstration Project area. *www.langholmproject.com*

19 On North Uist, during the summer, it is possible to see hen harriers from the C83 (known locally as the 'Committee Road') that runs from the west coast at grid reference NF768671 on the A865 to NF789729 on the north coast. Look out for small car park on the high section of the road. This is an excellent viewing location to see not only harriers but also short-eared owls, merlins and golden eagles. Nearby, enjoy the Balranald RSPB reserve where you will see merlin in winter. *www.rspb. org.uk/reserves/guide/b/balranald*

20 One of the best places to see harriers outside the nesting season is Galloway where many of Scotland's breeding hen harriers spend the winter. Wetlands and marshland are the places to look and an excellent starting place is Loch Ken near Castle Douglas by joining the Galloway Red Kite Trail (see Red Kite for details).

OSPREY

There are currently six visitor centres in Scotland offering live pictures and sometimes views of nesting ospreys. These are listed below (21-26) along with some places to view fishing ospreys:

21 From April through to August a visit to the famous Loch Garten Osprey Centre near Boat of Garten in Strathspey is a must. Tel. reserve office: 01479 831476 or visit *www.rspb.org. uk/reserves/guide/l/lochgarten/about.asp*

22 The nesting ospreys at the Scottish Wildlife Trust reserve at Loch of the Lowes, near Dunkeld, Perthshire (NO040435) are almost as well known as those at Loch Garten. For details visit *www.swt.org.uk/*

23 Ospreys are also nesting in the Borders in Tweedale. Viewing facilities have been set up at Glentress Forest, 2 miles east of Peebles on the A72, and at Kailzie Gardens, 2 miles south of the town on the B7062. For further details visit *www.forestry.gov.uk/ tweedvalleyospreys*

24 The private life of a nesting pair ospreys in Galloway is also being revealed with facilities at the Wigtown Wildlife Viewing Room, County Buildings, Main Street, Wigtown. *www.dgcommunity.net/osprey*

25 In the Trossachs, the David Marshall Lodge Visitor Centre at Aberfoyle offers live pictures of ospreys during the spring and summer months. Visit website for details. *www.forestry.gov.uk/aberfoyleospreys*

26 At the Caerlaverock wetland reserve near Dumfries, fishing ospreys are regular and during April to August there is CCTV coverage of a nearby nesting pair. *www.wwt.org.uk/caerlaverock*

27 For budding wildlife photographers, Rothiemurchus Estate offers a superb opportunity to watch and film fishing ospreys at their fishponds (NH898115) at Aviemore, Strathspey. For further details and booking please contact the Rothiemurchus Fishery on 01479 810703. *www.rothiemurchus.net/index.html*

28 The shallow tidal waters of Findhorn Bay on the Moray coast attracts fishing Ospreys from April to September and is especially good during the summer months. There is a car park and viewing hide off the B9011 Kinloss to Findhorn village road at NJ052632 or continue into the village and watch from the harbour across the narrows towards Culbin Forest. For those who enjoy walking *www.forestry.gov. uk/forestry/INFD-778JUG* provides details of access through this remarkable forest to the remote west side the Bay.

29 From early April to early September, the firths of northern Scotland are great places for fishing ospreys and the Beauly, Inverness and Dornoch Firths are well worth visiting, with the Cromarty Firth offering the best opportunity of a sighting. Try watching from the northbound lay-by on the A9 (NH592604) at the start of the Cromarty Bridge, which links the Black Isle with Easter Ross. Fishing ospreys are also likely at the north end of the bridge between Ardullie roundabout (NH587622) and Foulis Point visitor centre (NH599635) with an added bonus of seeing harbour (common) seals hauled out on the shore. Further north, on the A9 before you reach Golspie, stop in

the large lay-by at Loch Fleet – you may see ospreys hunting there.

PEREGRINE

Despite their relative abundance, Peregrines can be a difficult bird to see away from nesting areas. Disturbance during the breeding season can result in abandonment by the pair and the loss of any eggs and chicks. We therefore will not advertise any breeding location apart from three eyries where formal viewing arrangements have been made.

30 At Bin Forest (NJ496428), 3 miles northwest of Huntly, Aberdeenshire, on the A96, the Huntly Peregrine Wild Watch has been established in a partnership led by Forestry Commission Scotland. At one of their quarries, the fortunes of a nesting pair of peregrines can followed each year from April to September. Visit their web site *www.forestry.gov.uk/ huntlyperegrines* or phone 01466 760790 for further details.

31 South of Glasgow on the A73 is the World Heritage Village of New Lanark where the Scottish Wildlife Trust have a reserve at the Falls of Clyde. Peregrines breed here annually and there is a viewing facility. Visit the web site for details of visiting arrangements. *www.swt.org.uk*

32 At the Grey Mare's Tail, approximately 10 miles northeast of Moffat on the A708, there is a viewing cabin for watching nesting peregrines. A walk up the hill beside the spectacular waterfalls is an added treat. Visit the web-site and select Grey Mare's Tail from the property list. *www.nts.org.uk/visits/*

33 In the winter, many peregrines are attracted to estuaries and tidal mudflats, such as Aberlady Bay between Edinburgh and North Berwick where hundreds, sometimes thousands of wading birds and wildfowl congregate. The appearance of a peregrine overhead will create panic amongst the feeding shorebirds, which take to the air in tight swirling flocks, often rising to a great height to avoid the threat of a stoop. To the observant, these are the first signs of an approaching peregrine, which can often be seen perched on a prominent post or sometimes on open ground, resting between hunting bouts.

RED KITE

The easiest way to get spectacular views of Red Kites is to visit one of the four dedicated red kite feeding stations established in Scotland:

34 Argaty Red Kite feeding station. Situated on Argaty estate, near Doune, Perthshire. Take the A820 from the A9 or the A84 from Stirling to Callander. At Doune, turn north up King Street to Argaty. The project is well signposted. Booking is recommended, phone 01786 841373. *www.argatyredkites.co.uk*

35 The Red Kite Feeding Station, Bellymack Hill Farm, Laurieston, Castle Douglas, Dumfries & Galloway, DG7 2PT. Phone: 01644 450202. Off the B795 road. Red Kite feeding time is at 2pm daily. *www.redkitefeedingstation.co.uk*

36 Easter Anguston Farm, Aberdeen. Easter Anguston is located one mile west of the busy village of Peterculter on the outskirts of Aberdeen, off the A93 Banchory Road, and visitors are always warmly welcomed. *www.rspb.org.uk/community/blogs/aberdee nredkites/default.aspx*

37 The Tollie red kite visitor centre on the Brahan estate in Easter Ross, will be opening in March 2010. It is situated 2 miles from the Conon Bridge roundabout, just off the A832 Tore to Ullapool road. Feeding time in the winter is 2pm and it will be well signposted.

Away from the feeding stations, red kites can be seen at:

38 Trossachs Bird of Prey trail: this 25 mile circular driving route runs from Aberfoyle to Doune, and the varied and dramatic landscapes along its route offer the perfect habitat for up to 13 species of bird of prey to be seen. *www.birdofpreytrail.com*

39 Galloway Red Kite Trail: the trail is an anticlockwise route of some 24 miles around Loch Ken (winter) with an additional fourteen miles of forest drive (summer only). Being out on a bike is a great way to spot red kites and for the energetic, it's a reasonably level route, with cycle racks provided at Boat O Rhone, New Galloway and Mossdale. *www.gallowaykitetrail.com*

40 The Black Isle, Highland. Just north of Inverness, this is where in 1989, after an absence of 100 years, the reintroduction of red kites to Scotland began. Red kites have now spread across much of the Black Isle but are commonest in the western half. Birds can be seen from all major and minor roads that crisscross the peninsula.

41 Central Scotland. In west Perthshire, the A84 Doune to Callander road with parking available in lay bys and the A85 between Comrie and St Fillans are likely routes for seeing red kites especially about one mile west of Comrie. Alternatively, the B827 Braco to Comrie road over the Langside Moor (NN791138) is worth visiting.

WHITE-TAILED EAGLE OR SEA EAGLE

42 Loch Frisa, Isle of Mull, Argyll. *www.forestry.gov.uk/mullseaeagles* The Forestry Commission has established a hide overlooking a nesting pair of sea eagles. The rendezvous point for booked trips is at the south, or Aros, end of the Loch Frisa track. (OS Grid Reference NM 5440 4585). It is less than one mile up the track from the Lettermore junction of Loch Frisa forest track and the A848 Tobermory to Salen road. Trips to the hide run on Tuesdays and Wednesdays at 10.00am and 1.00pm. Please note these details are subject to change as the season progresses. You can make bookings through Craignure Information Centre on 01680 812556.

43 At the Aros Centre, Portree, Isle of Skye there is CCTV viewing of a nearby white-tailed eagles nest. Visit the web site for further details. *www.aros.co.uk*

44 Whilst on Skye, take a wildlife boat tour from Portree for spectacular views of white-tailed eagles that are attracted to the boat with fish bait. The web site has all the details. *www.skyeboat-trips.co.uk/destinations.asp*

45 Also on the Isle of Skye, look for white-tailed eagles from the viewing hide overlooking the Kylerhea Narrows, the narrowest sea crossing between Skye and mainland Scotland. Either take the summer ferry from Glenelg to Kylerhea or, from the A850 on Skye, three and a half miles west of the Skye bridge, take the road to Kylerhea and at the signpost, turn north on the small track to the Otter Haven car park at NG788222. *www.forestry.gov.uk/website/WildWoods.n sf/LUWebDocsByKey/ScotlandHighlandNoFo restKylerheaKylerheaOtterHavenCarpark*

46 Look for white-tailed eagles on Loch Maree, Loch Ewe and Gruinard Bay, Wester Ross, on a circular, all day drive through some of the most spectacular scenery in Britain. Leave the A9 at the Tore Roundabout on the Black Isle on the A835 (Ullapool). After Garve, turn left on A832 for Achnasheen and Kinlochewe. The road continues along the south shore of Loch Maree to Gairloch, Loch Ewe, Gruinard Bay and Dundonald rejoining the A835 at Corrieshalloch Gorge. Make frequent stops to search for eagles and take in the great views.

47 Both white-tailed and golden eagles occur on the Isles of Canna and Rum in the Inner Hebrides. Take a day excursion sailing from Mallaig on a Caledonian MacBrayne passenger ferry and explore these Hebridean gems. Visit the web site for timetable. *www.calmac.co.uk*

48 In Aberdeenshire, individuals have reached Loch of Strathbeg, north of Peterhead on the A90 where the RSPB have a large reserve and visitor facility. Check out *www.rspb.org.uk/reserves/guide/l/lochofstrathbeg/index.asp* Eagles have also made regular appearances at the Ythan estuary (NK002268) viewed from the A975 and the nearby Meikle Loch (NK029308) both north of Aberdeen.

49 The whole of the Tay estuary between Perth and Dundee is attractive to sea eagles and they can appear anywhere over this vast area. To the north of the estuary, in the Kilspindie/Rait area to the east of Scone, Perthshire, there is a footpath leading to a trig point on Pole Hill (NO195260). This is a great place to look for birds over the estuary or to see individuals heading for nearby roosts.

50 Some of the young eagles reintroduced to Fife have dispersed over a large area of Scotland but the majority are still in the east. They are attracted to estuaries and lochs where there are an abundance of waterfowl such as ducks and geese to hunt. The National Nature Reserve at Morton Lochs (NO461263) attracts sea eagles and the area is well worth a visit. Visit the web site for visiting arrangements. *www.tentsmuir.org*

The website of Irish white-tailed eagle reintroduction project is worth visiting for this gives details of released birds being satellite tracked, with many spending time in different parts of Scotland. *www.goldeneagle.ie*

BARN OWL

Being nocturnal, barn owls will be active throughout the night and often at dawn and dusk. When feeding chicks, they may have to hunt during the day to meet the demands of a growing family but it is in the winter when daytime hunting is more likely. At this time of year food can be much scarcer and the weather at night less favourable for hunting. Uncultivated fields, old meadows, rough pasture and marshland provide good hunting for a hungry barn owl. These are well worth watching at dusk, particularly if there are old farm buildings, an abandoned dwelling or hollow trees nearby. Barn owl sightings north of Inverness are of particular interest to us, as these are of the most northern breeding barn owls in the world.

51 There is a chance of seeing hunting barn owls in the Galloway Forest Park in Dumfries & Galloway. The web site has details of the park and the wildlife viewing opportunities on offer. *www.forestry.gov.uk/gallowayforestpark*

52 At the Wildfowl & Wetlands Trust reserve at Caerlaverock the private life of a nesting pair of barn owls is being monitored by CCTV cameras from March to September. *www.wwt.org.uk/caerlaverock*

53 Islay has a number of breeding barn owls that are often seen hunting during the day. The RSPB reserve is especially good for seeing them. See under Hen Harrier for visiting details.

Grasping a huge fish, the white-tailed eagle exploits its long, broad wings to get airborne.
Emblematic of centuries of struggles between birds of prey and people, this bird is returning to our shores.

ACKNOWLEDGEMENTS

We are grateful to the volunteer specialists in the Scottish Raptor Study Groups for developing our knowledge of birds of prey. We thank the following for specific comments on the text: David Jardine, Malcolm Ogilvie, Duncan Orr-Ewing, Andrew Stevenson, Patrick Stirling-Aird and Pat Thompson.

Professor Des Thompson was founder chairman of the Scottish Raptor Monitoring Group and is Policy and Advice Manager in Scottish Natural Heritage. He has published several books on birds.

Dr Helen Riley has been involved in a wide range of international and national bird conservation issues, ranging from albatrosses to raptors.

Brian Etheridge has a lifelong interest in birds of prey. He is the RSPB Red Kite Project Officer for North Scotland, and is Raptor Monitoring Officer for the Scottish Raptor Monitoring Group.

First published in Great Britain in 2010 by
Lomond Books Ltd., Broxburn EH52 5NF Scotland
www.lomondbooks.com

Produced by Colin Baxter Photography Ltd.   Copyright © Colin Baxter Photography Ltd 2010
Text Joint © Des Thompson, Helen Riley, Brian Etheridge & Colin Baxter Photography 2010

Pictures © 2010 All Rights Reserved by:
David Tipling: page 12; Laurie Campbell: pages front cover, 1, 4, 7 top, 11, 13, 15, 19, 21, 24, 25, 27;
Mark Hamblin: pages 2, 5 top, 6, 7 bottom, 8 bottom, 9, 14, 16, 17, 20, 22, 23, 26, 32; Markus Varesvuo / Nature Picture Library: page 5 bottom; Neil McIntyre: pages 8 top, back cover; Niall Benvie / Nature Picture Library: page 10;
Paul Hobson / Nature Picture Library: page 18; Peter Cairns: page 3

ISBN 978-1-84204-214-4   Printed in China

Front Cover: *Golden eagle*   Back Cover: *Osprey*   Page 1: *Kestrel*